JOHN

MARSHALLS

Marshall Morgan & Scott
1 Bath Street, London EC1V 9LB

Copyright © Marshall Morgan & Scott 1982

First published by Oliphants Ltd 1938
Reissued in enlarged edition 1953

Reprinted 1954, 1956, 1960
First issued in paperback in Lakeland series 1962
Seventh impression 1962
This edition 1982
Impression number 10 9 8 7 6 5 4 3 2 1

ISBN: 0 551 00945 4

Printed in Great Britain by Richard Clay (The Chaucer Press) Ltd,
Bungay, Suffolk

CONTENTS

HE WAS BORN

WHEN John Wesley came into the world that sunny June day in 1703, Queen Anne was *not* dead. It is very unlikely, though, that anybody troubled to tell Her Majesty that a fifteenth baby had arrived in the Wesley family, which already filled to overflowing that rambling old rectory away there in the little Lincolnshire market-town of Epworth.

Every home, including yours and mine, owes much to those who have lived in other homes two and three generations before, whose names and natures we inherit. That was certainly true of the Wesley family. For three generations at least their ancestors had been gentle folk by birth, scholars by training and clergymen by choice.

As the young Wesleys grew up they would hear things about Grandfather Wesley and Grand-father Annesley; and some of the children would be shocked, and some of them would be secretly proud that those two old stalwarts were each of them 'agin the government' of that day, and were turned out of their vicarages, one in Dorsetshire and one in London, because they would not 'conform' to laws made by those who wanted to interfere with the ways in which people should worship God.

"Yes, and they turned out *great* Grandfather Wesley from his vicarage, too, because he was a dissenter," said Mary impressively, one summer's day in 1713, as once again she told some of the old familiar family stories to the younger children sitting in the rectory garden. They always crowded around her to listen when she was in a story-telling mood.

"When you go to London perhaps Uncle Matthew will take you to Spital Yard, close to the Bishop's Gate in the City of London, and he will show you the fine tall house where Grandfather Annesley lived, and point out the very room at the top where every day he said his prayers and read twenty chapters of his Bible."

"Is that where our mother was born?" asked little Jacky.

"Yes, that was where she was born," replied Mary.

"And how old was she when she married our father?" asked Martha, who was the little sober-sides of the Wesley household.

"Nineteen," said Mary, "and father was twenty-six, when he was a curate with £30 a year, and soon after they went to their first real home at South Ormsby."

"Tell us again about father going to Oxford," coaxed Jacky.

"When he was twenty-one father walked to Oxford with exactly forty-five shillings in his pocket. He went to Exeter College as a 'poor scholar' so all through his student days to get his degree he had to work hard in the kitchen and in the servants' hall, as well as in the lecture room and in his study."

"I think it was worth it," said Jacky thoughtfully. "Some day, perhaps," the small boy went on, "father's book on Job will be finished and then he will be famous and have more money."

"Some day . . . perhaps," said Emily, the eldest sister, with a sigh. "But it is time you four children were in the schoolroom. Mother will be there in a minute and you know she is never late. Besides there are things to be done in the dairy. Come along, Mary—come along, Hetty."

It often puzzled the young Wesleys to think that they lived in a rectory belonging to the Established Church and that their father was a clergyman of the Established Church, and that though he had so many dissenting ancestors he was always at loggerheads with the dissenters there in the flat fen country round Epworth.

The generations had already brought some strange changes of faith and fortune to the Wesley family and there were more to come. Nobody at Epworth in 1713, least of all the autocratic little rector, ever dreamed that little Jacky, with the blue eyes, the long nose, and the auburn hair, would, forty years on, be regarded as the greatest 'dissenter' that England had ever known, and because of that he would be hated bitterly by some and loved tremendously by others.

And certainly nobody at Epworth or anywhere else ever dreamed that, more than two centuries after, the whole world, Anglican, Nonconformist, Catholic and all the rest would join in honouring the memory of John Wesley who began his life in the Epworth Rectory on June 17, 1703.

II

HE GREW UP AT EPWORTH

THE Wesley household at Epworth into which little Jacky was born in 1703 was an amazing one in many ways. People have said that the Wesleys were probably the brainiest family in England in that day. They were desperately poor, and yet each of the boys and girls in that home was well bred, well behaved and well educated.

Their mother, Susanna Wesley, beautiful to look at, fascinating to listen to, ordered her big family of children and servants in a very wonderful way. Everything was done according to rule and according to time. For instance, no Wesley baby ever had anything for which he or she cried. They were taught to cry softly, if they cried at all. Sometimes, it was Mrs. Wesley herself who supplied them with a good reason for crying—but always for their good.

The children were taught a delightful courtesy, very unusual in those days, toward each other and toward their servants and neighbours.

Another of Mrs. Wesley's rules was that on the fifth birthday of each of her many children she would take that particular boy or girl into a room away from the others and on that one day teach him or her the alphabet. Apparently this was successful every time. She was not only wife and mother and housekeeper at the rectory, but school-mistress too, for she was educated far and away beyond the average woman in her day. She did her work in that old rectory schoolroom so well that when her three sons went up to one or other of the great public schools of that day in London each did well. The girls too learned Greek, Latin and French from their mother, as well as how to order a house. All the children inherited from their father the knack of writing poetry.

Just before Jacky Wesley was six he very nearly lost his life. The old thatched rectory with its lath and plaster walls was burnt to the ground. In a very few minutes the place was like a furnace; all the family escaped except little Jacky who was sleeping by himself. His father was going to go up the burning stairs once again when they crashed to the ground in flames. The distracted rector knelt down to pray. At that moment his small son, roused by all the noise and the light of the flames, appeared at a window. There was no ladder anywhere, so one resourceful neighbour jumped on to the shoulders of another and they rescued the little chap just as the roof fell in. John Wesley often described himself when he grew

up as "A brand plucked out of the burning."
Doubtless, he had the Epworth fire in mind when
he used that phrase.

Samuel Wesley found it very hard work to
make both ends meet. His wife had to do most of
the pulling to make them meet. There was a time
when for a debt of £30 his creditors put the rector
into the Debtors' Prison in Lincoln Castle, but
even in that terrible place Samuel Wesley occu-
pied his time preaching to the other prisoners
and trying to improve their miserable lot.

It was a case of plain living and high thinking
in the Epworth Rectory. Very often the rector was
away on long, slow, expensive journeys to London
and Mrs. Wesley was in charge of the affairs of
the family and mostly of the affairs of the parish.
The curate who conducted the services at the
church was rather a poor tool and John Wesley
never forgot how his mother started services of
her own in the big kitchen at the rectory. Presently
some neighbours and friends also came to those
services.

With all these many things to do Mrs. Wesley
found time, or made time, to talk to each of her
children about God and about praying to Him and
pleasing Him. She used to have one evening for
each child. Thursday evening was Jacky's. All his
days he never forgot those wonderful talks with his
wonderful mother, and long afterwards, when he
was a don at Oxford, he wrote to his mother
begging her still to think of him on Thursday
evenings.

The ways of the Epworth Rectory then were very different from the ways in any home in our day. People have called Mrs. Wesley a Spartan mother. Perhaps she was. It was a Spartan age, but any home or any mother who could produce sons like the three Wesley boys, Samuel, John and Charles, is worthy of our respect and our reverence. Most people will agree that it is very poor taste to throw stones and mud across two centuries at the Epworth Rectory and the people who lived in it. Rather do we feel like lining up with the people who found a place for Susanna Wesley, representing all devoted mothers, in the stained glass window in Liverpool Cathedral dedicated to all noble women.

III

HE BECAME A CARTHUSIAN

ONE of the most interesting and historic spots in London today is Charterhouse. In its day it has been a monastery, an Elizabethan mansion, and then from 1611 the centre of a noble charity founded by Thomas Sutton. From that date it has been a place where eighty old gentlemen might end their days in peace and comfort, and where forty "poore youthes" of gentle birth might receive the best education that England at that time could give.

Samuel Wesley, the Epworth Rector, ambitious for all his boys, obtained from the Duke of Buckingham, the Lord Chamberlain of those days, a nomination to Charterhouse School for little Jacky. One day, when the boy was ten years old, the rector started off on his sturdy nag to ride to London with Jacky riding pillion behind him. The journey took four days. The boy was torn between two sets of feelings. He hated the idea of leaving the happy family life of the old rectory, and especially the idea of leaving his mother, and yet there was waiting for him the big adventure of life at Charterhouse and in London.

John Wesley never forgot that first trip from Epworth to London. The roads were rough, mere bridle tracks many of them; he shivered when he passed a tall gallows at a cross roads where dangled the bodies of some poor wretches who had been hung for stealing a few shillings. In the inns, where he and his father slept, he listened, terrified, to talk of highway robbers and footpads. He saw groups of rough-looking men going down side streets and side lanes with birds under their arms, and with a sigh the old rector told the lad about the evil and cruelty of cock-fighting and bull-baiting, and much else that marked and marred the country life in the England of the early seventeen hundreds.

In due time the father and son passed through the great double door of Charterhouse in London, and the little chap put on the knee breeches, the doublet and the baize-lined cloak of a "gown boy" and began his schoolboy life at Charterhouse. Before the rector left he gave Jacky his blessing, and as a bit of parting advice told him to run round the playground three times every morning, so that he might make himself hard and keep himself fit. John resolved to do this, and every morning, wet or fine, his long reddish hair flying in the wind, the little chap's nimble legs carried him three times round, and no amount of chaffing from the other "gown boys" interfered with his running, and he kept it up all through his Charterhouse days. When he was an old man of eighty, and still working tremendously hard and still wonderfully hale and hearty, he told people that he put it all down to the three laps round the Charterhouse playground. You can still see that spot when you look through the iron gates in Charterhouse Square which lead to what are today the Medical Schools of the famous Bart's Hospital.

In those days it was a rough and tumble life at Charterhouse. Probably there were then about sixty or seventy boys in the school. A good deal of bullying went on, and the bigger boys ate the food meant for the smaller boys. "I had little but bread to eat," wrote John Wesley in his later days, "and not great plenty of that."

But John Wesley got a sound education, one of the best that could be had anywhere in the land in that day. The classical languages were taught by the headmaster, and mathematics and science by his assistant.

John Wesley gave little trouble to anybody,

and when he got any half-holidays he spent them
with his older brother Samuel, who by this time
had got his degree at Oxford and was a master at
Westminster School.

Nowadays, Charterhouse is one of the great
public schools of England, housed in a great range
of buildings down at Godalming in Surrey. A por-
trait of John Wesley hangs in the School Hall. In
the cloisters of the old Charterhouse in London
there is a tablet unveiled in 1937 by the then
Archbishop of Canterbury to the memory of John
Wesley. It is difficult to think of any higher honour
that the School could do to an old boy. A former
and very famous headmaster has spoken of John
Wesley as the greatest of old Carthusians. How
well this is put in a Charterhouse School Song:

Wesley, John Wesley, was one of our company,
Prophet untiring and fearless of tongue,
    Down the long years he went,
    Spending yet never spent,
Serving his God with a heart ever young.

IV

HE HEARD ABOUT "OLD JEFFREY"

IT was while John Wesley was a "gown boy" at
Charterhouse that there were some very mysterious happenings at the Epworth Rectory and

he must have been very sorry not to have been at home and close up to all these strange goings on.

For six months, on and off, the bewildered rector and his family were regularly visited by a noisy ghost, or imp of mischief, who did the oddest things in the oddest ways at the oddest moments. There were mysterious raps on doors and walls, there were thumps beneath the floors. Sometime the family heard the smash of crockery, or a sound like a carpenter planing wood, or of a shuffling among the boots and shoes; or the rattle of chains, or the jingle of falling coins or the tread of feet.

After a while these noises became so familiar that they ceased to frighten anybody, and the lively girls of the rectory nicknamed the unseen but very audible visitor "Old Jeffrey."

More than once the indignant rector felt himself actually being pushed along the passages of his own house. He never lacked courage so in a loud voice he challenged the ghost, if it had something to say, to meet him in his study. The rector then walked off defiantly to that room in the rectory, prepared for a very unusual interview. Imagine his feelings when he found the door held against him!

After a while the girls discovered that they could make "Old Jeffrey" very angry by passing uncomplimentary remarks about him, suggesting that the noises they heard were caused by rats; whereupon the ghost would thump the walls and the floor more vigorously than ever.

Mr. Wesley pursued the noise into almost every

room in the house and even chased it into the garden. Determined to be master in his own house he obtained a mastiff. When, however, "Old Jeffrey" paid his usual nightly visit the newly acquired dog retreated ignominiously under the bed, howling and shivering with fright. The distracted rector talked about getting a gun and shooting the unwanted and unwelcome visitor, but it was pointed out to him that a charge of lead would not be likely to have any effect upon a ghost.

It should be added that "Old Jeffrey" could be one of the politest ghosts known to history. When he was on duty he would lift the latches of the doors as the girls approached to let them pass through. Mrs. Wesley, in her calm matter-of-fact way, appealed to the invisible imp not to disturb her after tea, when she always had her "quiet hour" and her wish was duly respected.

Various members of the Wesley family each in his or her own way, and in great detail, told and wrote this amazing story of "Old Jeffrey"; and a neighbouring clergyman, called in to assist in expelling the ghost, corroborated all the details that the Wesley family had given.

Nobody succeeded in explaining, or in explaining away, these mysterious visitations to the Epworth Rectory. The wisest among the friends and neighbours could only shake their heads and talk not about a ghost but about a *poltergeist*, but that was no explanation at all. As Dr. Fitchett, the famous historian, remarks "The evidence concerning 'Old Jeffrey', if it were given in a court of law, and in a trial for murder, would suffice to hang any man."

It is on record that a hundred years after the Wesley family had left their rectory-home at Epworth, the then resident rector also heard strange and alarming noises; so much so that deeming discretion the better part of valour he and his family took an extended holiday on the Continent.

No wonder that John Wesley, in later life, always had an open mind concerning ghost stories, many of which are recorded in his *Journal*.

V

HE WENT TO OXFORD

OXFORD, as everybody knows, has been a famous University ever since the twelfth century. It has had many ups and downs. When John Wesley left Charterhouse in 1720, at the age of seventeen, and went up to Christ Church as a commoner, the whole University was in a baddish way as far as its standards of morals were concerned. The students were for the most part a slack lot, far keener on drinking and gambling than on study and work. The dons took their salaries all right, but were willing enough to dodge their duty in the way of giving lectures and coaching their students.

It was into this sort of thing that John Wesley was pitch-forked at an age when nowadays most public school boys are still in the Upper Sixth preparing for the work that lies ahead.

For the first time John Wesley became his own master. What a young man does then is a pretty good indication of the sort of thing he will do later on, but thanks to the Epworth training and to the teaching of that wonderful mother of his, John Wesley at Christ Church lived a straight clean life. While others idled he worked, making the most of the opportunities that had come to him. He could not forget that his father, his grandfather and his great-grandfather had all been at Oxford before him, and it would have been a poor thing to have let down the family name and record, now that his time had come to take the best that Oxford could give, and to leave severely alone not only the things that were bad but also the things that were second best.

John Wesley made plenty of friends during this time at the University. He had a quick humour and a neat gift of making verses—grave and gay. He was the life of any party in which he found himself, and an ever-welcome guest in the homes of some of his fellow-students who lived nearby in the Cotswold villages.

It seemed a natural thing for John Wesley to do what so many in his family had done before him—to become a clergyman. He was tremendously conscientious about it all, and long letters went to and fro between Epworth and Oxford, as to the decision that had to be made.

He preached his first sermon in the little parish church of a remote Oxfordshire village near Witney, called South Leigh. Today a tablet recording that fact is to be seen in that interesting old church. In his old age John Wesley once went back to South Leigh, and he met one of the old parishioners who remembered that first sermon of his forty years before.

After John Wesley had obtained his Bachelor's Degree, and after he had spent some time assisting his father in Lincolnshire, he was appointed Fellow of Lincoln College: a position he held with honour to himself and to that College for a quarter of a century. Today, a visitor to Lincoln College seeing the Wesley bust, the Wesley rooms and the Wesley portraits, realises that high tribute is thereby being paid to its most famous son. It was just at that time that John Wesley began to develop into a prim and rather grim High Church-man, believing tremendously in all the forms and ceremonies of the Established Church, and disciplining himself just about as severely as some of those old monks who had lived in Charterhouse centuries before. He got up at four o'clock, he fasted regularly, he worked hard every waking minute, and strained even his strong body almost to breaking point. He visited the prisoners in the Oxford gaol, and prisons were terrible places in those days; he tried to brighten the lot of the inmates of the poor house and the mad house; he taught ignorant children who had nobody to look after them. Despite all this tireless religious activity and his preaching of carefully prepared sermons he could not help feeling that his was a fruitless sort of life. He drew no crowds. He influenced no lives. He touched no consciences. He warmed no hearts.

After a while John Wesley's younger brother Charles went up to Oxford, also to Christ Church, and with some other more seriously-minded students he formed an Oxford Group of those earlier days, which was contemptuously called "The Holy Club." They met to pray, to study the Bible and to talk over what they had been reading and thinking. They were very regular in their attendance at Communion Services, and some rather clever undergraduate of that day, wanting to poke fun at them, gave them a nickname. With sneering patronage he called them "Methodists." When this clever quip went the round of the college men rocked with laughter at the aptness of that word—"Methodists!"— "Splendid!" It just suited those young enthusiasts, the two Wesleys, and George Whitefield and Robert Kirkham and the rest. "Methodists!" What a joke!

Strange, don't you think, that the term which was scornfully applied in 1729 is one which two centuries later thirty millions of people, scattered all over the world, are proud to bear and are trying hard to live up to?

VI

HE BECAME A MISSIONARY IN GEORGIA

In the early part of the eighteenth century King George II was keen on the development of the American Colonies. Out in Georgia there was a pioneer settlement, made up of a very mixed lot of settlers, for which a chaplain was wanted. John Wesley heard about this and the idea of going to Georgia appealed to him tremendously. Ever since the Epworth days, when his mother read to him stories about the early Danish missionaries in South India, he had been deeply interested in missionary work. He imagined that if he went out to Georgia as chaplain, he would be able to attend to all his duties among the colonists, and then have quite a lot of time left to do missionary work among the Red Indians.

John Wesley wrote to his mother, who was a widow by this time, asking her if she approved of his going to Georgia as chaplain, together with his brother Charles, who had been offered the position of secretary to the founder and governor, General Oglethorpe. The plucky old lady wrote back, "Had I twenty sons I should rejoice that they were so employed."

So John Wesley started off for Georgia in October 1735, in the little sailing ship the *Simmonds*, being officially enrolled as one of the foreign missionaries of the Society for the Propagation of the Gospel.

Travelling to America then was a matter of months, not of hours as it is now. It was a slow journey, an uncomfortable journey and a risky journey. John Wesley had a full share of all the discomforts of that memorable voyage. More than once his ship ran into very heavy gales; huge seas broke over the little craft and time after time it seemed as if she would not weather the storm. John Wesley found himself face to face with death. He was quite honest with himself, and had to admit that clergyman though he was, he was afraid to die. This experience puzzled him, and so did something else. On board was a party of emigrant Moravians from Central Europe, who were also bound for Georgia. They were not in the least disturbed by the terrible storms and the possibility of their going down with the ship. They sang hymns and held their services day after day, whether it was blowing a gale or whether the sea was as calm as a millpond. The very fact that they were dissenters, yet so much braver than he was, set John Wesley thinking. He realised that they had a belief in God that he had never possessed, and he made up his mind to try to get it too. With this end in view he there and then started to learn German so that he might the more easily talk with the Moravians, hoping thereby to learn the secret of their simple faith and steady courage.

At last, the long long voyage was over and John

Wesley plunged into his work as chaplain to the young colony at Savannah. He arranged numerous services, he visited every home, he organised schools for the settlers' children, and ruled them with a strictness that was reminiscent of the Epworth schoolroom, without any of Susanna Wesley's other loving ways to relieve it. He tried to teach the Indians, but they did not in the least welcome his efforts.

He was tremendously busy, not at all popular, and all the time in the back of his mind he was searching for that wonderful courage-giving belief in God, which those Moravians had.

Meanwhile, Charles Wesley had managed to work up a big quarrel with the bluff old Governor, General Oglethorpe, with the result that the young secretary cleared off back to England.

Things went from bad to worse with John Wesley. Bigoted and tactless he got into everybody's bad books with his over-zealous activities among old and young. After less than two years in Georgia, John ignominiously followed his brother Charles back to England.

The Georgia adventure, begun with such high hopes, was a bitter disappointment. However, we can see now that it was all part of God's great plan to prepare John Wesley for work that lay ahead. Those two troublous years in Georgia taught that rather self-sufficient High Church don that there was some big thing that those simple Moravians had which had not yet come to him. To discover

a truth like that is always well worth while,
no matter what it may cost.

VII

HE SOUGHT FOR AN ANCHOR
THAT HELD

WHEN, on February 1, 1738, John Wesley
arrived home from Georgia and landed at Deal
he went straight to the trustees of the Georgia
settlement and handed in a full report of his
chaplaincy—and his resignation.

A few days after he put all his High Church
pride in his pocket and made his way to the
London headquarters of the Moravians. He
attended their meetings, he asked questions of
their ministers and talked with their members.
Just then there was in London a Moravian
missionary whose name was Peter Böhler. He was
a man after John Wesley's own heart—a scholar,
a bachelor, absolutely selfless and utterly devoted
to his missionary ideals. Like those other Moravians on that storm-beaten little sailing ship—
the *Simmonds*—Böhler was so splendidly certain
about the God he served, and the guidance and
gladness that came in that service.

John Wesley went doggedly to the Moravian
Meeting House. There were long talks and
longer arguments, and when later he reached
his lodging there were long hours that he spent

on his knees. John Wesley was desperately keen to have for himself that sure and certain belief, "assurance" people called it, that he knew was to be had and yet could not get.

No man or woman, or boy or girl has ever persevered on such a quest as that without at last finding what was sought, and John Wesley's search was at last rewarded. He read again and again the story of St. Paul's conversion, and prayed that to him too there might come a blinding flash, and with it an assured belief that he was an accepted servant of Christ his Saviour.

Meanwhile, Charles Wesley was going through an exactly similar experience. Despite the fact, that like his brother John, he too was an ordained clergyman, he was very conscious that he was not an out-and-out believer in Christ. He also was searching, he also was in touch with the Moravians, and he also was trying to save his own soul and the souls of other people by his own desperate activities and ministry among prisoners, criminals, paupers and the like. It was just as if these two brothers were trying to lift themselves nearer to Heaven by their own strong arms and strong wills.

Charles Wesley was the first to find what he was seeking, and in the end it came in such a simple, almost casual way.

He was utterly worn out with his many activities and anxieties, and while he was recovering from an attack of pleurisy in his humble lodging with a certain Mr. Bray, a brazier who lived in Little Britain, near Aldersgate Street, a servant in the house, a good religiously-minded girl told her master that she was sure their lodger was in trouble about his soul. Being just a servant maid she could not at first summon up enough courage to say anything to a *clergyman*.

One day she spoke to him through the keyhole of his bedroom door. "In the name of Jesus Christ arise," she said, "and thou shalt be healed of all thy infirmities."

Charles Wesley, wearied and worried, took these words, uttered under that strange impulse by that simple servant girl, as a message to him direct from God. In a flash there came to him that "assured belief" that he sought.

In a second he *knew* that his "sins" were forgiven, he *knew* that he had the love of Jesus actually in his own heart, he *knew* that God would take charge of his life and all that he would have to do was to obey.

All this happened on Whit-Sunday, May 21, 1738, whereupon, Charles Wesley, the best poet of all in that family of poets, wrote a hymn, the first line of which was:

Where shall my wondering soul begin?

The second verse goes on:

O how shall I the goodness tell,
Father, which Thou to me hast showed?

That hymn, which has an honoured place in every Methodist Hymn Book, has been sung over and over again by other seekers down through the years who at last have found the precious thing that came to Charles Wesley that day.

VIII

HIS HEART WAS STRANGELY WARMED

JOHN WESLEY began the day on Wednesday, May 24, 1738, one of the most miserable men in London. He had had a restless, wakeful night. It worried him tremendously to know that there was this big thing in life—this assured belief about God—that his friends had, but which despite all his desperate efforts he could not get.

"What is it that hinders?" he kept asking himself, and his mind was busy trying to find out whether it was something more that he had to give, or something more that he had to get, or something more of both.

By five o'clock that morning he was up and dressed, and once again he prayed and prayed and read and re-read his Bible. One particular passage stood out as if in big type and greatly cheered him, and that was "Thou art not far from the kingdom of God."

Later in the day he decided to go to the service in St. Paul's Cathedral. He climbed those many

steps and entered through that great door.
Possibly some people that day noticed the pur-
poseful tread of the neatly-dressed little clergyman
as he walked up the aisle, and took a seat where he
could hear the singing and follow the service.

"Out of the deep have I called to Thee," sang
the choir. It caught the very mood of John Wesley
at that moment. "Lord, hear my voice," went on
the choir, and John Wesley continued that prayer
in the silence of his own heart.

By the evening of that day John Wesley felt
tired and lonely. He knew that there was to be a
meeting that night in a little room somewhere in
Aldersgate Street, but he felt altogether too miserable to go. However, he made the effort, and on
reaching the Aldersgate room he dropped on to a
bench just as a man was starting to read Luther's
Preface to the Epistle to the Romans. Nobody is
quite sure whether it was read in English or Latin
or German. Of course, it would have been all the
same to John Wesley whichever it was, as he
could have followed it in all those languages, and
indeed in a few more. At any rate, the actual
passage was almost certainly about the Holy
Spirit, which to quote Luther, "doth make us
new hearts, doth exhilarate us, doth excite and
inflame our heart that it may do those things
willingly of love which the Law commandeth."

John Wesley listened to every word. Then the
Holy Spirit had a part to play in the getting of
this assured belief. In other words, God also was
waiting and wanting to do something. It didn't all

depend on what John Wesley was trying to do. Why that was the very solution of the whole problem! Why ever hadn't that dawned on him before?

It was like coming out of the cold mists into God's own sunshine. It warmed him through and through—heart and all. At last, at last John Wesley had found the key that unlocked the door. He *did* believe and now it was for him just to love and obey. How simple it all was when he saw it like that.

That "assured belief," why, he had it. His prayer had been answered. It had come as it came to St. Paul, in a flash. His heart was bursting with this new love. "It doth exhilarate," Luther had written. John Wesley there and then handed himself over to God. His sins, of which he had repented so bitterly, did not matter now, they were taken away. From now on he was God's child and he kept telling himself that his part was to love and to obey.

Later that night he wrote in his *Journal* a calm summary of the happening of that wonderful day.

"About a quarter before nine . . . I felt my heart strangely warmed. I felt I did trust in Christ . . . An assurance was given me that He had taken away *my* sins . . . I then testified openly to all there what I now first felt in my heart."

The "heart-warming"—lovely phrase—happened that night. "Conversion," some people call it, putting the same thing into a single word.

The name matters little, the experience matters much.

John Wesley wanted not only to testify to the people in that Aldersgate Street room, he wanted right away to tell the glorious news to his brother Charles, who was still ill at his lodging only a few minutes' walk away.

Charles Wesley could understand it all because the very same experience had come to him only three days before. He told his brother about the hymn he had written, he read it over to him and then the two of them, with their friends joining in, sang for the very first time:

Where shall my wondering soul begin?

Methodism, our Methodism, was being born just then and it was born in song, the song of two men, who believed and who knew that their sins were forgiven and who there and then handed themselves over to God, determined from that moment to believe, to love and to obey.

IX

HE TOOK TO PREACHING IN THE OPEN AIR

ANYBODY who knows anything of the state of England two hundred years ago will agree that the two Wesleys, after the thrill of their heart-warming in May 1738, had about as stiff a job as any men ever undertook to make any impression on the people who in that day lived either in London or in the country.

Everything was wrong, from the Court and Society at the top to the drink-sodden men and pitifully starved women and children at the bottom. The latter lived like pigs in their filthy hovels and insanitary slums. They died like flies, with the people around them, high and low, caring as little as if they were cattle or vermin.

Gambling was a national vice, every sixth shop in London was a gin shop, there were over 160 different "crimes" for which people could be hung. Temple Bar was all the time "decorated" with human heads, the pillory and the whipping post were found in use almost in every village.

With a few notable exceptions the Church of that day did little to fight these terrible evils. There was no "good news" proclaimed from the pulpits, only good advice given, and that from clergymen who preached but did not practise. It was an age which had a horror of enthusiasm, and yet it would need a spiritual revolution to alter such a condition of things in the life of any people in any age.

God, at that point in history, called the two Wesleys, John and Charles, to be His revolutionaries. They both heard His voice, they had an assured belief about that and, with every power they possessed, they both started in to "obey!"

After the heart-warming they preached in the parish churches of London in a way which alarmed the vicars and curates and churchwardens. People, rough, ignorant and even criminal, flocked in great crowds to hear them. The message they gave was so simple, so direct, and so convincing, that men and women, who felt the blackness and the burden of their sinful lives, cried out in their agony of shame and repentance. The two Wesleys told them about God's spirit meeting them half-way, and they passed on their watchwords, "believe, love, obey."

As was to be expected, all this outraged the easy-going clergymen of that day. They didn't at all like having their churches filled to the doors with unwashed hordes of people, who wept and cried out to God as the Wesleys preached their convincing sermons and made their persuasive appeals. Of course they would have had to admit that the preaching of the two brothers made thieves honest, drunkards sober and cruel men gentle and kind. Still it was all so very irregular, and there was such a horrid display of unforgivable enthusiasm. No, the only safe thing was to close the church doors in the faces of these too-zealous young men, and that was what they did.

Everybody should remember that both John and Charles Wesley liked to have things done decently and in order. They loved the Prayer Book with its litany and its collects and its well-ordered services. But what were they to do now, seeing that the message they knew they had to give could not be given inside the parish churches? The only thing to do was to preach in the open air—an absolutely unheard of thing in those far-off times.

It was their friend of "Holy Club" days, George Whitefield, who began it. A couple of hundred people listened open-mouthed to this young clergyman in bands and gown as he preached to them in a way they had never heard any man preach before. Next time there were two thousand people in George Whitefield's open-air congregation, and very soon twenty thousand, and, thanks to Whitefield's magnificent voice and compelling message, everybody in that vast crowd heard him and not a single one of them heard him unmoved.

John Wesley followed in the footsteps not only of his friend, George Whitefield, but it comforted him to think that he was also following in the footsteps of his Master, Christ, when he stood bareheaded in the market-place, or on the village green or in any open space and gave His message of good news. He didn't like it a bit at first. "I submitted to be more vile," he wrote; "standing on a little grassy mound I preached to a great crowd." Very soon both John and Charles Wesley, like George Whitefield, were preaching in the open air to great crowds of people and with the same wonderful results.

All of which was a still greater shock for the bishops and clergymen of that day. More irregularity! More enthusiasm!

The three friends, sharing in the thrill of this new adventure, found themselves caught up in something bigger than themselves, and they marvelled at what God was enabling them to do, now that they were living out their promise to love and to obey.

x

HE BECAME AN APOSTLE ON HORSEBACK

WHEN John Wesley took to preaching in the open air, soon after his "heart-warming," he little thought that he was starting something which was to occupy him for a full fifty years, but so it was.

John Wesley paid more turnpike tolls than any man that ever rode the roads of England. He certainly was better known throughout the length and breadth of the land than anyone in his century—kings and queens included. How he gathered those huge crowds that hung breathless on his words, and gathered them so quickly, remains a mystery, and especially so when we remember that those were days when the telephone and the telegraph, and indeed the penny post, had not been invented.

The amazing energy of this "preaching friar" of the eighteenth century is realised when we hear that he preached over 40,000 sermons, an average of fifteen a week, and that he covered at least a quarter of a million miles on foot, on horseback, or in the post-chaise, which later on in his life one of his friends had given him. He moved up and down and across England according to a fixed plan. Somebody has said that he knew the roads, rough and smooth, from London to Newcastle and from London to Bristol just like a city postman knows his round.

He lived like a soldier on active service, lightly equipped, ready to be in the saddle or on the march at a moment's notice.

He was fit, he was fearless, he was resolute. He preached in any building, large or small, that was available, and where there was none to be had he preached out of doors in any spot where folks could gather. He was always willing to preach to a congregation of one, if any other horseman overtook him as he went ceaselessly up and down those rough roads of two hundred years ago.

When he was riding alone, John Wesley rode with a slack rein so that he might read. That was how he kept up his wide studies and made his many sermons.

His suit and cloak might be threadbare, but they were always tidy and neat. Anybody could see at a glance that he was a gentleman. Although he was in the open air so much he had a complexion that a schoolgirl might envy. He wore his hair long, and scorned the artificiality of a wig. People who knew him well have left it on record that he had dark blue eyes and, as we should expect, a firm chin. His spare frame had the strength of steel, he could stand up to an amount of fatigue which would have killed most men. He would walk his thirty miles a day, or ride eighty, if need be, and at the end of the journey be as fresh as when he started.

Earl Baldwin, who had such rich Methodist blood in his veins, paid a fitting tribute to the tireless work and widespreading influence of John Wesley. His words are worth reading more than once.

"When we read history," said Earl Baldwin, "we find a great deal two hundred years ago about politics, kings and battles, but very little about John Wesley. Yet as the years go by historians have begun to say that it was the lives of men like Wesley and Whitefield that really were the significant factors in moulding the character of the people, and it is largely owing to the spirit which they breathed throughout England that the immense impetus was given to the reform which took place in the country during the last century."

XI

HE RECRUITED A COMPANY OF "ROUGH RIDERS"

JOHN WESLEY had a very tidy mind. He loved things to be done decently and in order. Up to the time of the "heart-warming" he was all for services in the parish churches, conducted according to the Anglican Prayer Book, and, of course, it was unthinkable that anybody should preach who was not duly ordained as a clergyman.

When there came to John Wesley that great vision of the world as his parish, he very soon saw that to undertake and overtake the great task of carrying the good news of the Gospel right through the land he would have to enlist some irregular forces, as well as the regular ones; so he began to appoint carefully selected men as lay preachers.

John Cennick, the first of this splendid band, led a life as devoted as John Wesley himself. He "burnt out" at the age of thirty-seven and lies in the Moravian Burial Ground at Chelsea. Thomas Maxfield, whose name is second on the list, actually started to preach before John Wesley gave him permission. Wesley, hearing this, journeyed in hot haste from Bristol to London to stop him, but found, as his far-seeing mother told him, that this young man clearly had a call from God to preach, every bit as much as John Wesley himself.

One by one others were added to this corps of "rough riders," and they proved exceedingly useful in many ways. They prepared the way for their great and tireless leader, they worked under him and with him, and they carried on when he moved to another centre.

They were poorly paid, poorly clad, poorly equipped and poorly housed, but they had the courage of heroes. "We enjoyed great poverty and great peace," said one of them very simply. They covered vast distances, mostly on horseback and sometimes on foot. We can the more readily understand this when we hear that in 1746, John Wesley divided the whole of England into seven circuits. Peter Jaco, for instance, was appointed to the Manchester circuit, which took in Cheshire, Lancashire, Derbyshire, Staffordshire and part of Yorkshire. Think of what that involved in the way of tireless travel over the roughest of eighteenth-century roads. Many a day he rode his horse thirty to forty miles, preaching three or four times in different places on the way, and at the end was thankful to have a little clean straw as his bed.

These "rough riders" of John Wesley faced the bitterest persecution. Mayors and magistrates scolded them and sometimes imprisoned them as "pestilent fellows." Often rowdy mobs, incited by people who ought to have known better, interfered with their open-air services and pelted them with stones, rotten apples and turnips, and filth of every kind—"the cudgels of Satan" as one man quaintly put it.

"My head was broken with a blow," wrote Thomas Lee, "but I never found my soul more happy." It was this same indomitable soul who at the end of his days said triumphantly that if all the hardships of his life as one of John Wesley's travelling preachers were spread out before him, he would pray, "Lord, if Thou wilt give me strength, I will now begin again."

No wonder these "rough riders" were invincible. Like John Wesley himself they denounced in no uncertain terms the evils of the day—smuggling, drunkenness and worldliness. They stood alone in market places and on village greens, and gave their message in just the same way as their great leader did and with the same results.

Their wives were just as heroic. Desperately poor, despised by their neighbours, continually on the move, left alone to manage their large families, these pioneer preachers' wives deserve a place of honour all their own in the thoughts of Methodism these two centuries after.

John Wesley enlisted into his regiment of "rough riders" bakers, stonemasons, miners, labourers, troopers in the King's army as well as a few who had more education and a higher position in life.

Those were the men who helped to establish the Methodism that we all enjoy so happily and so comfortably to-day. We do well to honour the "fathers that begat us," and to stand at the salute as John Wesley and his regiment of tireless horsemen go riding by. Surely some who hear their story will want to catch their spirit, and carry on their work and so lay the foundations for bigger and better things still in days to come.

XII

HE POSSESSED THE COURAGE
OF A "V.C."

LET nobody imagine that John Wesley's many
journeys and innumerable services were carried
through without fierce and bitter opposition. The
outraged clergy were against him; the low-living
gentry set on their servants and tenants to
interrupt his meetings; and the riff-raff were
enraged almost to the point of madness by his
fearless rebukes and straight talking.

John Wesley was a man of dainty, almost
fastidious taste. We can only faintly imagine what
he must have suffered when time after time dead
cats, rotten eggs and decaying cabbage stalks
were hurled at him, and with no uncertain
aim.

Angry mobs, often encouraged by people who
should have known better, actually sought his
blood. To them it was just as good fun to bait a
Methodist preacher as to bait a bull. Probably
there is hardly another record of such human
brutality being met by such superb human
courage.

Nothing can illustrate this better than John
Wesley's own words.

"I rode to Falmouth . . . Almost as soon as I

was set down, the house was beset on all sides by a multitude of people . . . The rabble roared . . . 'Bring out the Canorum! Where is the Canorum?' (an unmeaning word which the Cornish generally use instead of Methodist). No answer being given, they quickly forced open the outer door and filled the passage. Only a wainscot-partition was between us, which was not likely to stand long. I immediately took down a large looking-glass which hung against it, supposing the whole side would fall in at once . . . Poor Kitty cried out, 'O, sir, what must we do?' I said, 'We must pray' . . . . She asked, 'But, sir, is it not better for you to hide yourself?' . . . I answered, 'No. It is best for me to stand just where I am.' Among those without were the crews of some privateers, which were lately come into the harbour. Some of these . . . set their shoulders to the inner door, and cried out, 'Avast, lads, avast!' Away went all the hinges at once, and the door fell back into the room. I stepped forward . . . and said, 'Here I am. Which of you has anything to say to me? To which of you have I done any wrong? To you? Or you? Or you?' I continued speaking till I came, bare-headed as I was (for I purposely left my hat, that they might see my face), into the street, and then . . . said, 'Neighbours, countrymen, do you desire to hear me speak?' They cried . . . 'Yes. Yes. He shall speak. He shall. Nobody shall hinder him'."

Again and again, in his *Journal*, John Wesley calmly and without comment or complaint tells the story of the abuse and persecution he encountered. Listen to this:

"I made haste to Goston's Green, near Birmingham, where I had appointed to preach at six (a.m.), but it was dangerous for any who stood to hear, for the stones and dirt were flying from every side, almost without intermission, for near an hour. I afterwards met the Society and exhorted them, in spite of men and devils, to continue in the grace of God." And listen to this:

"I rode to Wednesbury. At twelve I preached near the middle of the town to a far larger crowd than was expected. I was writing in the afternoon when the mob beset the house. We prayed that God would disperse them; and it was so. Before five the mob surrounded the house in greater numbers than ever. I desired one to take their captain and bring him into the house. After a few sentences interchanged between us the lion became a lamb. I desired him to go and bring one or two more of the most angry of his companions. He brought in two who were ready to swallow the ground with rage but in two minutes they were as calm as he. I then bade them make way that I might go out among the people. As soon as I was in the midst of them, I called for a chair and, standing up, asked 'What do any of you want with me?' I spoke a few words which God applied, so they cried out with might and main: 'This gentleman is an honest gentleman and we will spill our blood in his defence'.

"Later that day a mob of opponents from Walsall came pouring in like a flood and bore down all before them. The Darlaston mob made what defence they could, but they were . . . outnumbered, so that in a short time, many were knocked down, the rest ran away and left me in their hands.

"To attempt speaking was vain. They dragged me along until . . . seeing the door of a large house open I attempted to go in, but a man, catching me by the hair, pulled me back into the middle of the mob. I continued speaking all the time and asked 'Are you willing to hear me speak?' Many cried out: 'No, no! Knock his brains out! Down with him. Kill him at once!' Others said, 'Nay, but we will hear him first.' I continued speaking for above a quarter of an hour and I broke out aloud into prayer. And now the man who just before headed the mob turned and said, 'Sir, I will spend my life for you: follow me, and not one shall touch a hair of your head'. Two or three of his fellows confirmed his words and got close to me immediately.

"A little before ten God brought me safe to Wednesbury; having lost only one flap of my waistcoat and a little skin from one of my hands."

Nowadays, some people are fond of long words and clever sounding phrases, and talk about "mob psychology." John Wesley did not use that term, but he knew better than most how to quiet an uproar and to calm a crowd. He never faltered or flinched. He possessed a courage which came to him from his great Captain, who also counted His life not dear unto Him and who also endured valiantly to the end.

XIII

HE BEGAN TO BUILD CHURCHES

WHEN John Wesley found that practically all the parish churches of the land were closed against him, he was not prepared to take it lying down. He decided to build a "preaching house" as he called it, where he could hold services and do a lot of other things besides. The first of many that were to follow, was the "New Room" in the Horsefair, Bristol, a city which in those days came next to London in importance.

It is very interesting to look back from today, where there are in round figures 100,000 Methodist Churches or preaching places scattered all over the world, to that day in May 1739, just a month after his first service in the open air, when John Wesley laid the foundation stone of his "New Room" in Bristol. He designed the building himself, and very cleverly too. It was a place where services were held, and there was a schoolroom where neglected and ignorant children were gathered and taught. There was also a little vestry where the "society" met on week-nights. Small though that vestry was it was big enough in 1745 to hold the eleven members of the second "Conference of the People called Methodists." A number of bedrooms were included in the scheme so that Wesley's preachers could be accommodated, and a larger room was provided where a common meal could be served for quite a number of people. There was also a stable for a couple of horses.

Thanks to the generosity of the late Mr. Edmund S. Lamplough the "New Room" was in 1930 restored, and its interest greatly added to, by the placing in the forecourt of a superb life-size statue of John Wesley on his horse. Hard by is the very stable into which he so often led his tired horse. This earliest of all Methodist preaching places can be seen today very much the same as it was two hundred years ago, when John Wesley was so frequent a visitor.

John Wesley's second big building enterprise was in London. The Royal Foundery in Moorfields, London, was blown to bits in 1716, many of the workmen losing their lives in the explosion. For many years the ruins were a stark and ugly reminder of that terrible tragedy. They were reached by a narrow lane which also led to the kennels where the Lord Mayor kept his pack of hounds, hunting being then a regular pastime of the City Fathers.

Moorfields was a wide space where the citizens of London walked and watched the sport of their apprentices. During the summer of 1739, John Wesley regularly preached there in the open air. Somebody suggested that he should take over the old roofless Foundery and make it his "New Room" in London. He had a tremendous lot on his hands just then, and very little money available, but very bravely he resolved to tackle this enterprise too, and he held his first service in the reconditioned Foundery on November 11, 1739. He used it as his London headquarters for nearly forty years, and out of the old ruins he made a preaching place that would hold fifteen hundred people, a set of rooms for himself and his travelling preachers, a coach house and stable, a book room, a dispensary, a school, an orphanage and an almshouse. It was the rule at the Foundery that everybody, John Wesley included, sat at the same table and had precisely the same food as the old people who lived in the almshouses.

The bell in the little belfry rang every morning at five o'clock for a preaching service, at which the sixty children from the orphanage were always expected to be present! Mrs. Susanna Wesley spent the last two years of her life, happily and serenely, at the Foundery, and it was to the same place early in 1751 that John Wesley brought his wife when he married so very unexpectedly. Unlike the "New Room" at Bristol the Foundery has completely disappeared. Not a single stick or stone remains, though some of its backless benches and its beautiful lectern are still preserved at City Road Chapel for interested people to see.

John Wesley proceeded to take over certain churches in London which were derelict just then, including several which originally belonged to the Huguenot Refugees, and he preached regularly in Spitalfields, Seven Dials and Southwark, to growing congregations of devoted and devout folk. All over the land Methodist preaching-places sprang up, and John Wesley kept in close touch with them all, visiting them himself as often as was possible.

City Road Methodist Church was opened in 1778, nearly forty years after John Wesley began to preach in the Foundery. It is still known as "Wesley's Chapel" and thousands of Methodist people, young and old, from near and far, go there as a tribute of respect for the life and work of the man whose heart was strangely warmed in Aldersgate Street on May 24, 1738. There can be few visitors who do not return to their own particular church, one of the 100,000 of today, without resolving to take back in their own lives something more of John Wesley's selfless service and untiring devotion. Thoughtful people will remember that he was the human founder not only of the "mother church" of Methodism, but of a world-wide movement, with its many millions of members in every corner of the globe. The world has indeed become the "parish" of the indomitable man who lies buried in that God's acre in City Road, but whose spirit goes marching on.

XIV

HE BEGAN TO BUILD A CHURCH

IT is one thing to work with just one group of people in one particular place. It is quite another thing to extend that work to other people and to other places. It was in that more difficult task that John Wesley was so supremely successful. He saw the wisdom of using the services of other people, who had caught his spirit, both men and women, and who, under his leadership and inspiration, were prepared to win others for the way of life that had brought peace and joy to their own hearts.

John Wesley had a creative mind with plenty of ideas of his own. He would also catch hold of the ideas of other people and use them in such a way that they led to something really big and important. For instance, at Bristol the loyal little company which met in the "New Room" were formed into groups and each was to pay a small sum every week toward the cost of their new preaching place. Several people volunteered to go round to the homes of these good folk and collect these weekly pence. Then it was discovered that it saved a lot of time for the collectors if all the members of the group brought their money once a week to the man or woman who was to receive it. "A capital idea," thought John Wesley. "I'll make those collectors into 'leaders' and their groups shall not only be little companies of people paying their weekly pennies, they shall be 'classes' for the instruction of the members in the Christian way."

It really is an amazing thing that John Wesley's scheme, evolved in this simple fashion, has been carried on for two hundred years and in many lands.

As the work grew, John Wesley saw that it was going to be something far bigger than could be directed and controlled by himself and his brother and the few Anglican clergymen who joined them, so he began to use the services of lay preachers. Some of these were set apart and maintained by and for the work. Others preached on Sundays but carried on their usual jobs on the other days of the week. They were a marvellous lot of men, whose lives are well worth studying, and whose courage and devotion are well worth imitating.

John Wesley, in his ceaseless journeys up and down England, and indeed right through the United Kingdom, kept in close touch with all that was being done and with all who were helping in the doing of it. He encouraged his people to build their own preaching places, often enough plain little chapels tucked away in back streets. Each of them became a new and living centre for the missionary work of winning other people to a new and better way of life, which was the special feature of Methodism in its earlier days. More and more hearts were warmed, more and more people came "to believe, to love and to obey."

John Wesley always remained an ordained clergyman of the Established Church, and he liked to think of all his Methodist followers as a "society" inside that Church, and yet by his very acts and by his own hand he deliberately cut, one by one, the ties which bound him and his people to the Church, as by law established in the England of that day. For instance, he preached anywhere and everywhere, asking no man's permission; he authorised lay preaching, and himself ordained preachers and gave them the right to ordain others; and toward the end of his life, he licensed his "preaching places" under the Toleration Act as Dissenting Chapels.

With his logical mind, John Wesley must have foreseen what the result of all this was likely to be. Probably he hoped and prayed that the Established Church itself might alter, and when he saw no signs of this, no doubt, he trembled as he realised that he was giving Methodism a form which would inevitably mean that his "society" would grow into a Church. He could hardly have imagined that some day it would become the largest Protestant community in the whole world. We can be quite sure that if any such dream had come to him he would once again have said, very humbly, "It is the Lord's doing, and marvellous in our eyes."

XV

HE WENT TO CORNWALL

THERE was one corner of England for which John Wesley had a specially warm corner in his heart and that was Cornwall away in the extreme West. He visited Cornwall more than thirty times. Suppose we follow him along those Cornish roads, into the Cornish towns and villages and go with him into some of the homes in which he stayed, remembering that what happened there also happened in many other Counties and corners of England.

It all began when word came to John Wesley at the New Room, Bristol, brought by a Methodist sea captain returning from a coasting trip in his little cockleshell of a craft, that down at St. Ives there were a little company of men and women who met regularly to pray and to read the Bible and to help each other to live a life more like that of the great Pattern-life of their time and of ours. In those days St. Ives was quite an important place with a population equal to that of Liverpool at the same date.

The people who lived in Cornwall, being very remote from the rest of England, were for the most part ignorant, lawless and degraded, appalling drunkenness was rife, smuggling went on all round the coasts, and in some places, though probably not in as many as some people suppose, the inhuman practice of wrecking sacrificed the lives of brave sailors at sea to the greed of evil men on shore. The Cornish people earned some sort of a living, usually a very poor one, as miners or fishermen or farmers and all the wretched ways of life that belonged to the eighteenth century were to be found in Cornwall in abundance.

John Wesley knew all this, and although Cornwall then was a rough place, with rough people in it, that did not prevent him from wanting to help the place and the people. His first act was to send off "Brother Charles," on horseback of course, to discover whether the group at the strategic centre of St. Ives was likely to join up with the other Methodist Societies that were springing up here and there, all over the land.

The report must have been encouraging because a few weeks later John Wesley decided that he would himself visit St. Ives and he sent off two trusted helpers, John Nelson and John Downes to be his advance agents. Only one horse could be spared from the little stable at the New Room, so Nelson and Downes, had to travel "ride and tie." It was a long tiring journey and they had many adventures on the way, notably one at Digory Isbell's cottage "with the stone porch" at the tiny hamlet of Trewint, on the edge of the Cornish Moors.

The Cornish roads of that day were said to

be the worst in all England. Highwaymen and
footpads were plentiful.

John Nelson, like John Wesley kept a Journal
and in it he gives some details of the scanty
comfort experienced by these three Methodist
travellers on their first journey to Cornwall.
He writes:—

"Mr. Wesley and I lay on the floor; he had
my great coat for his pillow, and I had Burkitt's
Notes on the New Testament for mine. One morning about three o'clock, Mr. Wesley turned over
and finding me awake clapped me on the side
saying 'Brother Nelson let us be of good cheer,
I have one whole side yet, for the skin is off
but on one side'."

In those days, of course, there were no tele-
phones, no telegraphs, and no postal facilities
as we know them today, and yet John Wesley
was able to gather a crowd of not just a score or
two of hearers, but of hundreds and thousands.
He lived the life of a soldier, ready for instant
action, prepared to travel light and to travel
hard, *very* hard.

One of John Wesley's favourite preaching
places in Cornwall was Gwennap Pit which he
visited thirty-five times. This Pit is shaped like a
huge basin and is thought to have been caused
by a subsidence of the ground under which there
had been mining operations.

John Wesley's estimates of the number of
people who came to Gwennap Pit to hear him
preach may have been somewhat exaggerated

but without doubt many many thousands gathered there again and again. An interesting sidelight on one of these Gwennap Pit services is given in a letter from one of Wesley's early preachers who refers to the fact that "there were a thousand horses there and a thousand ragged small boys to hold the horses."

These open air services were not short by any means. They were held even when the weather was unfavourable. John Wesley wrote in his *Journal* in 1751: "It blew hard and rained almost without ceasing, but the congregation stood as if it had been a fair summer's evening." Several times he recorded, with wonder and gratitude, that his voice carried "to the skirts of the congregation."

Since Wesley's day Gwennap Pit has been tidied up and tier above tier of grassy seats circle the pit from top to bottom. Every Whit Monday some thousands of Methodists still gather for what is always an inspiring preaching service, with, as it seems to many, the spirit of John Wesley hovering near.

Another incident connected with John Wesley's visits to Cornwall must come into the story. Peter Martin lived to be over a hundred years old. He never tired of telling the story of what happened to him when he was a post-boy at a Cornish inn and had to drive John Wesley to St. Ives. When they reached Hayle river the tide was partly in so that in crossing the water drenched Mr. Wesley, in fact the horses had to swim for it.

Peter Martin naturally was greatly alarmed. John Wesley, unperturbed himself, wanted to give the lad courage. "Driver," he asked, "what is your name?" "Peter, sir," said the white-faced lad through his chattering teeth. "Fear not, Peter, we shall not sink," said John Wesley. They reached Lelant in safety and went on to St. Ives where John Wesley preached to a great crowd in his wet clothes, but this was only after he had seen that Peter was cared for and the horses rubbed down.

When in 1789, at the age of eighty-six, John Wesley paid his last visit to Cornwall he was received with almost royal honours. As he passed through towns and villages people filled the streets to see him once again.

It was on that last visit that he wrote in his *Journal* very humbly and very gratefully "Forty years' labour has not been in vain. There is a fair prospect in Cornwall from Launceston to the Land's End."

XVI

HE LOVED BOYS AND GIRLS

So many people think of John Wesley as an austere, ascetic. middle-aged or elderly man, always far too busy to care much about boys and girls. Even if he had the time to do so, so some

folk imagine, he lacked any inclination or apti-
tude to make them his friends.

Such a mental picture is quite out of focus.
You see John Wesley was himself a member of
that big, happy, lively family which made the
Epworth Rectory famous for all time. The
Wesley's were poor but polite and they were
polite to each other. They learnt how to make
their own fun without having much money to
spend in making it.

When he was ten years old John Wesley went
to a great public school and for half-a-dozen
years knew all about the rough-and-tumble life
where there was plenty of both.

All through his long life John Wesley looked
back with gratitude to his early privileged years
in his own home and to his later privileged
school days, and he went out of his way in London,
in Bristol and in other places, to provide, and to
get other people to provide, homes and schools
for the untaught, the unloved and the uncared
for. Thousands of children had to thank him for
food and shelter and at any rate for some education which is so very much better than no
education at all.

In his ceaseless journeyings all over England
John Wesley became the best-known visitor to
any town or village through which he passed,
and children would always be on the look-out for
him and when he appeared their shrill cries of
welcome would serve to announce to all and
sundry "Mr. Wesley has come." Children listened

fascinated when, in gown and cassock, he took his stand in some public place and began to preach. If they did not understand all that he said they sensed that such preaching and such a preacher were something and somebody strange and wonderful. In later years as they listened they looked with awe at his long silver-white hair, blowing in the wind, as he preached.

John Wesley showed his interest in boys and girls by doing what scarcely any other preacher did in those days. He would arrange special times when he could meet by themselves the children in any town he was visiting. Concerning one such meeting he wrote in his *Journal* "I expected twenty but we had fourscore, all of them wanting, many desiring, instruction." Then, as always, boys and girls knew an understanding friend when they met one.

John Wesley was always willing to do a service to any grown up and to any child. When the parents of little Constance Edmonds wanted to arrange for her to go from Land's End, at one end of Cornwall, to Tavistock, just over the border of the other end of Cornwall, it was quite natural for them to suggest that she should ride pillion behind Mr. Wesley as he made that quite considerable journey on horseback. One wonders what the great man and the little girl talked about. We can be quite sure that Constance never forgot that journey and probably, years afterwards, told her children and grandchildren all about it again and again.

At the New Room, Bristol, there is to be seen a very special five-shilling-piece, a coin which to-day's money could not buy. The story has come down to us that John Wesley used to stay with a family at St. Just called Chenhalls. In that house there was a small boy—William Chenhalls. John Wesley wanted to show his appreciation of the kind and generous hospitality he had received and also to encourage the lad who, it seems, was very well-behaved, so the visitor decided that he would give his host's son a tip. John Wesley did not search in his purse for the smallest coin to be found there, probably a groat (4d.). Not a bit of it. Nor was a shilling thought suitable. The preacher took out the largest coin in circulation in those days, a very handsome freshly-minted coin, as it happened, viz. a silver crown piece. That particular five-shilling-piece was never spent. Let us hope that young William did have some groats and shillings for himself, but the actual silver crown, the gift of John Wesley, was treasured as a souvenir in the Chenhalls family and was handed down from eldest son to eldest son until it came into the hands of Mr. Rosewarne Chenhalls whose daughter gave it to the New Room at Bristol where hundreds of boys and girls in these days, see it and realise that John Wesley knew how to be splendidly generous to a boy two hundred years ago.

Toward the end of his life a friend of John Wesley's, a well-to-do lady, wanting to take care of him, since he never took care of himself, gave him a chaise in which to make his journeys. It was just like John Wesley to block up one side of the chaise and turn it into a travelling study and bookshop. Nor did he keep that chaise to himself, since it was almost as rare a vehicle in those days as a motor car was a century or so later. He was more than willing to share it with other people, especially with boys and girls, so he told his coachman always to put in the horses and bring the chaise round to the house where he was staying half-an-hour before he was due to start on his journey. The children of the place, not being at school, since there were no schools for most of them to go to, could be relied upon to be there in a crowd to see their friend depart. It was John Wesley's instruction that they were to be allowed to get into the coach in batches and to go for a short ride, until the time came for the preacher to start off on the next stage of his ceaseless journeyings.

"I met the children," wrote John Wesley once, "this is a work which will exercise the talents of the most able preacher in England." That is how he regarded work among boys and girls, and he was never tired of telling them, as he told the grown ups, that the thing they had to do was "to believe, to love and to obey."

XVII

HE HAD A SPLENDID HELPER
IN DR COKE

WHEN John Wesley was seventy-three he felt that
he was facing increased work with decreasing
strength and that he needed an assistant. His
amazing life of tireless activity was drawing to
its close, though a few more years of service were
given to him. These he also used to the very full
in establishing on a firm foundation the work of
the Society he had founded.

He needed an assistant to keep in touch with
the rapidly expanding work not only in England
but in Ireland, in America, in Canada and in the
West Indies. He often prayed for a helper whom
he could trust absolutely, a man familiar with
his own ways of work, and sharing his own ideals
of selfless service and ceaseless evangelism.

God had such a man ready for such a task.
His name was Thomas Coke. He was the son of a
well-to-do apothecary in the little Welsh town of
Brecon. He went up to Oxford at the age of
sixteen and in due course took his Arts degree to
which later was added the degree Doctor of Civil
Law.

When Thomas Coke returned to Brecon he
qualified and practised as a lawyer and he was
so much thought of by his neighbours and friends

that while still in his twenties he was four times mayor of Brecon. Then he surprised everybody by deciding to become a clergyman and, after a while, he was ordained and became curate at South Petherton in Somerset.

Thomas Coke was not at all satisfied with himself or with his ministry or message. One day he had a long talk with a farm-labourer, who was a follower of John Wesley. That talk altered Thomas Coke's whole life and gave him new vision and a new mission. He began to preach in the Parish Church in such a way that there was a revival in that little Somersetshire town. The services were so crowded that the curate, at his own expense, put a gallery into the Parish Church.

All this enthusiasm upset a lot of people and they sent for the absentee vicar, telling him that he must come back and deal with his altogether-too-zealous young curate. This he did. The mob, incited by people who ought to have known better, marked the dismissal of the dead-in-earnest preacher by the continuous ringing of the church bells. Thomas Coke was turned out of the parish in ignominy.

It was not long after this that Dr. Coke linked himself up with John Wesley. The latter fell in love with the ardent young Welshman at first sight. Here was the right man appearing at the right moment and into John Wesley's *Journal* there went the entry: "I had much conversation with him and a union then began which I trust shall never end." Prophetic words!

Forthwith Thomas Coke started in to supplement the labours of John Wesley, first of all in Ireland and then in other places, with the result that Methodism rooted itself more deeply and firmly in many old and new centres.

In 1784, at Wesley's request, Thomas Coke went to America to assist the indomitable Francis Asbury and his brave colleagues in their difficult task of re-establishing the work of the Methodist Churches which had been so sorely upset by the American War of Independence.

A year later, and Wesley was eighty by this time, Thomas Coke was asked to make a second voyage to America, a long and tedious undertaking in those far-off days. He took with him three stalwart Methodist preachers who were to do pioneer work in Nova Scotia and in the West Indies.

That adventurous voyage is an amazing story in itself. It ended not in America but in the West Indies and led to the actual start of the organized work of the Methodist Missionary Society.

Later Dr. Coke returned to England aflame with the story of the success of the missionary work in the West Indies.

In those days of small ships and long voyages Dr. Coke crossed the Atlantic on his missionary errands no less than eighteen times and always at his own expense.

He lived to see no less than twenty-seven missionaries at work in the West Indies, with a church membership of sixteen thousand.

He died tragically at sea in 1814 on his way to found yet another Methodist mission to Ceylon and Java.

It was not for nothing that discerning people called Dr. Coke "the Christopher Columbus of Methodism."

XVIII

HE CARED FOR THE NEEDY

ENGLAND was anything but "a green and pleasant land" in John Wesley's day. There were a few people who were very rich, there were many who were comfortably off but there was a very large part of the population unemployed or if employed, shockingly underpaid and therefore desperately poor. They lived in insanitary hovels, their children were ill-fed, ill-clad and for the most part uneducated. Old people had to work and to work hard, as long as they had any strength left to work in them. Boys and girls, almost as soon as they could walk, were sent out to work for long hours in the mines or in the fields to earn a few coppers.

Drunkenness was rife and even the savage laws of those days did little to check the dishonest ways of men and women made desperate by their need for food and shelter and clothing and the other necessities, let alone the decencies, of life.

John Wesley from his undergraduate days had never turned a deaf ear or a blind eye to the needs of those less fortunate than himself. He lived frugally that he might give the more to the needy. At Oxford he gladly became the teacher of boys and girls who but for him would have had no teacher at all.

Before John Howard began his agitation for prison reform John Wesley had made a practice of visiting those foul places with very foul and unlovely people in them.

John Wesley enthusiastically supported Hannah Ball when, at High Wycombe, she started her first Sunday school in Methodism. It was another Methodist lady who brought the new development to the notice of Robert Raikes, of Gloucester, who soon became the means of starting hundreds of Sunday Schools all through the land. In those schools in those early days ignorant children received not only religious education but they were also taught to read and to write.

As, later, Wesley's work widened he started and arranged, for others to carry on, all kinds of activities for those who needed sympathy and help. At the New Room in Bristol, and at the Foundery in London, he started, on a modest scale of course, orphanages where children were cared for and educated. On those same crowded premises at the Foundery he managed to find room for some old women and arranged for them to be cared for in a Methodist atmosphere. He started a public dispensary at the Foundery and actually dispensed medicines himself. Although not a doctor he published a little twopenny pamphlet giving simple recipes for the more general complaints. Encouraged by the success and usefulness of this booklet he expanded it into a book which he called *Primitive Physick*. Pamphlet and book make quaint reading today but at that time they let light into very dark minds concerning some of the ills that flesh is heir to.

Strangers' Friend Societies were formed in various centres. Gifts of money and clothing, of food and fuel, were collected from the more prosperous among the Methodists and these were taken to the homes of those who were ill or desperately poor. Often a sick visit led to scrubbing the floor or washing the clothes of the person visited, emphasising the truth that cleanliness is next to godliness.

A "Lending Stock" was also started at the Foundery for honest folk who wanted temporary financial help. A few pounds were advanced in such cases to be repaid later, no interest being charged.

Perhaps most needy of all, two centuries ago, were those millions of shamefully wronged men, women and children who had been torn from their homes in Africa, by inhuman traffickers in flesh and blood, to be sold as slaves in America and the West Indies. When Wesley read of their sufferings his blood boiled and with a burning pen he wrote on this subject and his pamphlet

Thoughts on Slavery (much of which which was "borrowed" from an earlier Quaker writer) aroused much attention and helped to bring emancipation as he intended that it should.

It was to reach the needy, that John Wesley took on the, to him, unwelcome task of preaching in the open air when he was no longer welcomed in the Parish Churches of the land. He made up his mind that the whole world should be his parish so he was ready to preach anywhere at any time to any needy people willing to hear his message.

A churchyard wall, the steps of a market house, a sheltered meadow, the balcony of a merchant's house, a stone trough in a farm yard, an upstanding rock on a wide moor—all these ordinary and extraordinary places served John Wesley for a pulpit. He preached in cassock and gown, sometimes at four and five o'clock in the morning, and at every other hour of the day. He wrote concerning one of his open air services "the moon shone bright upon us."

Though in the earlier years enemies disturbed his services the common people heard him gladly. His gospel met their need. But let nobody imagine that at any time during his long life service for his great Captain was easy for this gallant soldier and servant. John Wesley had the spirit of a true crusader. He wrote: "If a dinner ill-drest, a hard bed, a poor room, a shower of rain—I do not repine." That was how he faced life. He himself splendidly lived up to the advice he gave his people:

"Do all the good you can.
By all the means you can.
In all the ways you can.
In all the places you can.
At all the times you can.
To all the people you can.
As long as ever you can."

XIX

HE DISCIPLINED HIMSELF AND THEN OTHERS

JOHN WESLEY had seen in his own home at Epworth, with its scanty resources and its many claims, that it pays all the time to have order and method in all the affairs of life. That was why he stuck to his early morning "three times round" at Charterhouse, and why at Oxford he experimented to find out how much, or rather how little, sleep he really needed so that he might usefully employ all the other hours of each day.

Quite deliberately he once wrote, "Leisure and I have taken leave of one another. I propose to be busy as long as I live." Somebody has said that he weighed out his time as a chemist weighs out his drugs.

He was fond of making rules for himself and for his own way of life, and he was extraordinarily good at keeping them, which is quite another thing. He was simple in all his habits, a small eater and a vegetarian. In his study not a book was out of place and no scrap of paper was ever left loose on his desk.

When he became the leader of his new Methodist movement, his naturally orderly way of living and thinking was immensely useful to him, and to everybody around him. He planned out his journeys with the greatest care. He ordered his own life by a daily time-table, which in this less strenuous age leaves us gasping. He conducted a personal correspondence so wide and so regular that we wonder how it could have been sustained by a man who never employed a private secretary, and who certainly never used a typewriter. Then there were the numberless other activities that filled John Wesley's life. He wrote pamphlets, he edited a magazine, he revised a whole library of worthwhile devotional works, and then published them at the cheapest possible price, so that his people, most of them without the educational privileges that had been his, might be instructed in the wisdom of the ages and in the ways of the saints.

He kept a *Journal* which today is a classic in English literature. He balanced his accounts to a penny and never had any muddle with his many and various financial enterprises. He spent as little as possible on himself so that he might give as much as possible to other people. He lived up to the advice that he was always giving to his followers, "gain all you can; save all you can, give all you can." He taught his people to have his own horror of debt.

"Though I am always in haste," he said, "I am never in a hurry." His amazing steadiness and the absence of all fuss in his methods and movements were infectious and gave courage and calm to the people around him, and that at a time when those qualities were specially needed.

John Wesley had a profound belief in himself, and in his own judgment, and he did not by any means welcome any interference with his decisions and directions. He was without doubt an autocrat, but never with a view to using his power merely for his own personal advantage.

"Believe, love, *obey*." Any man who obeys God, who obeys his own conscience, who obeys self-imposed and carefully drawn up rules for the order of his own life, has a right to expect obedience from those who are working with him and under him.

John Wesley, though thoroughly self-controlled and infinitely patient, never suffered fools gladly. He could "tick off" anyone who differed from him as neatly and as finally as any man who ever lived. Most of his followers and friends accepted all this readily enough, realising that John Wesley was usually right, and that when they did not agree with him they were usually wrong. There were some who kicked over the traces, and who parted company with John Wesley and with Methodism, but few of these thereby did much good for themselves or for other people.

An autocrat, a benevolent autocrat, and an autocrat for the glory of God, John Wesley in the very exercise of the power that came to him exacted obedience from other people, just as he himself sought in things great and small to render obedience to the great Master whom he loved and served.

XX

HE WROTE, EDITED AND CIRCULATED BOOKS

JOHN WESLEY was a scholar. That means that he grew up and lived all his life in an atmosphere of books. It also meant that when he found himself at the head of a great new religious movement he naturally wanted books to play an important part in shaping it, in developing it and in propagating it.

It takes one's breath away to learn that John Wesley himself wrote close on three hundred books and pamphlets and on subjects as varied as theology, history, logic, science, medicine and music.

In addition to this, with tremendous skill, energy and enterprise, he condensed and published in a handy pocket size fifty volumes making available the masterpieces of devotional literature to all who had a taste for them.

He published scores and scores of cheap pamphlets giving his candid forthright views on current events and these had a great effect on public opinion. These were "tracts for the times" long before the official Tract Societies came into being. Other pamphlets served to supplement his sermons and their purpose may be gathered from such titles as "A word to a Drunkard," "Swear not at all," "Remember the Sabbath Day."

During his lifetime he produced and circulated over twenty million copies of his various publications, large and small. He made a profit on all this of over £30,000 devoting the whole of this sum to religious and charitable purposes.

Somebody aptly said of John Wesley "he was the best gatherer and scatterer of useful knowledge of his century."

He not only daringly pioneered in the production and editing of books, he was equally original and skilful in his methods of circulating them. He filled the saddle-bags of his preachers with books and pamphlets and wherever they went with their spoken word they left behind his printed word. They were not only itinerating evangelists they were itinerating booksellers.

Presently, Wesley set up his own Publishing House which today is a vigorous and valuable asset to modern Methodism.

Remember, all this amazing activity in writing editing and circulating books was done by a man who every year preached 500 sermons, travelled 5,000 miles and had a saddle for his study.

To John Wesley books were tools, weapons,

produced for a purpose and that purpose was the winning for his great Master of the souls and minds, yes and the bodies, of all whom he could reach.

John Wesley hated controversy and yet all through his long life he was called on to defend himself and his methods and his Methodism from attacks by friend and foe. This he could do vigorously enough and with equal vigour he could himself go forth to wage wordy warfare against any evil no matter how strongly entrenched. His gift of simple forceful language, his logical mind, his dauntless courage and his utter disregard for his own reputation made him a formidable opponent. As Dr. Fitchett says "in his hands a pen had the deadly swiftness of a rapier."

John Wesley's three chief works, his *Notes on the New Testament,* his *Fifty-three Sermons,* and his *Journal,* together with Charles Wesley's successive collections of hymns, were mightily used to make their newly established Methodism a force and a factor in the land far beyond their faith or expectation. In the days when these volumes appeared books were few and expensive, and they had an immense sale and exerted an influence far and wide, among rich and poor, learned and unlearned.

Nor should these and other famous products from the virile and versatile pen of John Wesley, be left on dusty shelves unread by the present generation. In them there is guidance, stimulus, inspiration for us as there were for those for whom they were published two hundred years ago.

"He being dead yet speaketh"—with his rich mind, out of his warmed heart and by his inspired pen.

XXI

HE SAW GOD'S SEAL SET UPON HIS WORK

SOME people work hard and work long, and at the end sometimes wonder whether they have done very much after all. No disappointment of this kind came to John Wesley after his "heart-warming." He was not the kind of man to have his head turned by success or his heart broken by failure. He went serenely on, putting all he knew into all he did and, man of simple faith that he was, he was continually being surprised at the success that crowned his efforts. "This is the Lord's doing and marvellous in our eyes," those words of the Psalmist were constantly on his lips, reflecting the feelings in his heart as there reached him now one and then another evidence of more victories won over evil and opposition by his preachers and by his people, as they grew in influence and in numbers all over the land.

He saw wonderful success following the method of Church government that he had devised. Societies, classes, leaders, stewards and Conferences, these worked well throughout the British Isles, and eventually far beyond, for John

Wesley's work was not confined to his own country. It spread overseas to America, and the story of the part in that which Philip Embury and Barbara Heck played is well worth re-telling.

Embury was a young Irish carpenter who was converted in one of John Wesley's services. He became a local preacher, and after a while emigrated to America. Later on, Barbara Heck, another Irish Methodist, joined the party in New York. She was disappointed to find that Philip Embury had not started services there. One day she found him with some friends playing cards. This was too much for the strong-minded Barbara, she snatched up the pack of cards and threw the whole lot into the fire, giving Philip a piece of her mind. "You should spend your time preaching the Gospel, not playing cards," she said with some vigour. "How can I preach?" said Embury rather feebly. "There isn't a chapel to preach in, and there isn't a congregation to preach to." "Then preach here and preach to us," said the downright Barbara, and there and then, in that strange way, the first Methodist preaching service in America was held.

A little later there came along a certain Captain Webb, an English barrack-master stationed near New York. He too was a local preacher, and went into a pulpit, uniform, sword and all, and preached with an earnestness and an eloquence that would have delighted John Wesley's heart.

The work of these Methodist pioneers was so successful in America, that they wrote home to

England and asked to have some whole-time preachers sent out to them, offering if need be to sell their coats to provide the necessary funds. Of course John Wesley could not refuse such a request, and Boardman and Pilmoor were sent out in 1769, with £50 in their pockets to Christianize a continent! Today, there are in America 40,000 Methodist Ministers and over 50,000 Methodist Churches.

It is a poor thing to boast about anything, and a *very* poor thing to boast about anything connected with God's work. Let us at all costs avoid doing that in connection with the growth of Methodism in England, or in America, or anywhere else. No; John Wesley has shown us a better way and given us a better word. We do well frequently to have it on our lips—"What hath God wrought?"

XXII

HE HAD A GREAT GIFT FOR FRIENDSHIP

SOME men have the greatly-to-be-desired gift of attracting to themselves the friendship of other people. John Wesley had that gift in a marked degree. He showed it during his undergraduate days at Oxford. We can see it during that memorable voyage to Georgia, and in certain other directions during his stay in Savannah.

When, after the "heart-warming," he began his life work for Methodism, he made hosts of friends in all walks of life. Aristocrats and intellectuals received him on terms of equality. His poorer followers, and some of them were very poor, when they received him into their humble homes, found him appreciative, considerate and grateful. He was the perfect guest because he was the perfect gentleman. People talked about such visits for weeks after they had taken place, and for months ahead they looked forward to the next. Down in Cornwall, where toward the end of his life the warm-hearted Methodist people were specially fond of John Wesley, there were those who built on a special room to their houses to accommodate John Wesley, or any of his travelling preachers. At one cottage in the little hamlet of Trewint, near Launceston, there is still to be seen the "prophet's chamber" and the prayer room built by Digory Isbell for the use of John Wesley and his preachers, a very human link with the happenings of two hundred years ago.

The story of John Wesley's friendships would fill a book. For instance, there was Martin Madan, a clever young barrister and a great mimic, who once went to hear John Wesley preach so that he might amuse his friends by coming back to them and taking him off. "Prepare to meet thy God," were the words he heard when, rather late, he entered the building just as John Wesley was announcing his text.

The man and his message completely captured Martin Madan and when, later, he met the friends, who were looking forward to some clever fun at the expense of the Methodist preacher, the young barrister said simply, "Gentlemen, he has taken *me* off," and he re-preached to them John Wesley's sermon. Later he became a Methodist preacher himself, taking no stipend, and helping in many ways, including that of writing hymn-tunes, one of which is in our Methodist Hymn Book, though his name is not given as the author.

Another of John Wesley's staunch friends was bluff old Silas Told, a sailor with a very shady past. He was persuaded to go to the Foundery, with the result that he and his wife were soundly converted. John Wesley was a very shrewd judge of men and he thought he saw a likely school-master in old Silas, so he tried him out, and for seven years the one-time sailorman taught and loved the orphan boys at the Foundery, and on top of all that gave a tremendous lot of time to visiting and comforting the prisoners at Newgate.

It was a wealthy friend of John Wesley, Miss Lewen of Leytonstone, who gave him the post-chaise, which from that time on became almost as well known throughout England as John Wesley himself. The new owner of the chaise, always ingenious and always industrious, devised an ingenious folding desk and had it fitted inside the chaise.

John Howard, the wealthy country gentleman

who became the great prison reformer, was also
a friend of John Wesley. They thoroughly under-
stood and appreciated each other.

In his old age, at his house in City Road, John
Wesley received a visit from William Wilberforce,
then a brilliant young M.P. beginning his
memorable fight for the abolition of slavery,
which John Wesley, years before, had described
as "that execrable sum of all villainies."

Last to be mentioned in this list, but by no
means least in importance and in influence, is
the Countess of Huntingdon, a blue-blooded
aristocrat, and in that day a familiar figure in
Court circles. She became a great supporter of
George Whitefield and of John Wesley. She
often invited Methodist preachers to her beautiful
mansion, Donington Park, and gathered her
neighbours and friends to hear them preach.
This led to quite a revival of religion among the
aristocratic circles in which the Countess moved,
and it is on record that its influence reached
King George himself. This lady is said to have
spent £100,000 of her own fortune in founding a
college and in building chapels. Some of the
latter continue to this day, and are known as the
"Countess of Huntingdon's Connexion."

John Wesley was always a welcome guest,
anywhere, being full of anecdote and story. It
was the great Doctor Johnson himself who
described him as a "good conversationalist."
As one clever pen put it—"peers, poets, painters,
physicians, philosophers, prisoners; scholars,

statesmen, soldiers"—John Wesley met them all. He was always just himself, always God's servant, and always trying to get men and women "to believe, to love and to obey."

XXIII

HE MADE METHODISM "A NEST OF SINGING BIRDS"

UP to the time of the coming of the Wesleys, all the singing in the parish churches was the droning of the psalms in a drowsy atmosphere by a dreary-voiced choir. John Wesley set himself to alter that. He had no use for sour godliness. Taking full advantage of his brother Charles's wonderful gift of hymn-writing, he brought out first one hymn book and then another. These set the whole country singing the Gospel message on weekdays and on Sundays. He himself, like all the Wesleys, had more than ordinary poetic skill, and he used it in translating into English quite a number of hymns by the great German hymn writers. They stand there today in our present Methodist Hymn-Book, a solid foundation for the faith of a Christian, and amply justify the claim, not only of Charles Wesley, but also of John Wesley, to a front-rank place among English hymn writers.

There were hymns in all the usual metres

used by poets. There were other hymns, notably
by Charles Wesley, in metres that were daringly
original. We can imagine the popular appeal of
lines like these, set to a tune full of life and
movement:

> What a mercy is this,
> What a heaven of bliss,
> How unspeakably happy am I;
> Gathered into the fold,
> With Thy people enrolled,
> With Thy people to live and to die.

And like these:

> My God I am Thine;
> What a comfort divine,
> What a blessing to know that my Jesus is
> mine.

There were plenty of high-brow people in
that day who in a superior way talked about
jingling rhythms set to jangling tunes. However,
these joyous outbursts survived all criticism, and
will be first favourites far and near for yet another
century and beyond that.

There were other hymns from the inspired
pen of Charles Wesley which have become
classic and are now to be found in all the hymn-
books of all the Churches—"Gentle Jesus,
meek and mild," "Jesu, Lover of my soul,"
"Soldiers of Christ, arise," "Love Divine, all

loves excelling," and "O for a thousand tongues to sing." Charles Wesley had a hymn, and more than one, for every mood and every moment. He provided those familiar favourites, "Christ the Lord is risen today," for Easter, and "Hark! the herald-angels sing," for Christmas. Those who have counted say that he wrote over 5,000 hymns, an amazing output of an amazing genius. No wonder that quite recently an authoritative voice has said that the hymns of the Wesleys rank in devotional literature with the psalms.

It really is astonishing to discover how gifted in the matter of hymn-writing John Wesley's earlier helpers were. John Cennick, for instance, the first lay preacher in Methodism, wrote that beautiful evening hymn:

> Ere I sleep, for every favour
> This day showed
> By my God,
> I will bless my Saviour.

It is to Cennick, too, that we owe the two graces so often sung at Methodist tea-meetings: "Be present at our table, Lord," and "We thank Thee, Lord, for this our food."

Thomas Olivers, another of John Wesley's heroic "rough riders" (the man who rode 100,000 miles on the horse that he bought at Tiverton for £5), wrote that stately hymn which we so often sing: "The God of Abraham praise."

John Bakewell, yet another of Wesley's itinerating preachers (an educated man with some means of his own), was the author of "Hail, Thou once despisèd Jesus!"

John Wesley never claimed to be a musician, but he had an instinct for fitting the hymns he wanted sung to tunes that made people want to sing them. A popular air, a sailor's shanty, or anything else that came along, John Wesley used them all to win a way for the message of Methodism to the hearts and homes of all sorts and conditions of people.

XXIV

HE HAD ADVENTURES AND MISADVENTURES

JOHN WESLEY's *Journal*, which he carefully kept for so many years, records all sorts of happenings that came to him during his many travels. Other stories about him were told, and treasured, and have come down to us through the years, and we all hope that not a single one of them will be lost to Methodism in the days still to come.

John Wesley was very fond of that rather dull little Lincolnshire town in which he was born, probably because of its association with his mother. He was at Epworth on a certain Sunday,

and he offered to help Mr. Romley, the clergyman in charge, who, as it happened, owed his
position in the Church to John Wesley's father.
Mr. Romley flatly declined the well-meant offer,
and added insult to injury by preaching on the
Sunday morning against the Methodists and
all their ways and works. John Wesley did not
lack staunch friends in Epworth, and a certain
Mr. Taylor was very angry at the ungrateful,
un-Christian attitude of the vicar. Standing in
the churchyard afterwards, this good man,
presumably having obtained John Wesley's
consent, announced that Mr. Wesley, not being
allowed to preach in his father's Church, would
preach in the churchyard that evening at six
o'clock.

Practically the whole population of Epworth
turned out that night to hear him, and the
problem was, where could John Wesley, short in
stature, stand so that everybody could see and
hear him? He decided to stand on the flat
tomb-stone resting on the grave of his father,
who had died seven years earlier. That great
crowd of Epworth neighbours and friends never
forgot that impressive sight and that impressive
sermon, and John Wesley's own comment was
that he did far more good preaching from his
father's tombstone than he had ever done when
he was his father's curate and preached in his
father's pulpit.

John Wesley was always ready to be an
attentive listener and a reverent worshipper in

any parish church when he was free to attend a service. On one such occasion the local vicar sent his clerk to the pew of the neatly dressed, distinguished looking young clergyman, and asked him to preach the sermon, which John Wesley did, hearing afterwards that this particular vicar, had only a few Sundays previously denounced "that vagabond Wesley" in no uncertain terms.

Some people have suggested that John Wesley was without a sense of humour. Other people do not agree, and they can tell story after story in support of their view. On one occasion John Wesley heard that a certain infirmary had refused admittance to a sick man because he was a Methodist. John Wesley said impressively, "I will be avenged on them!" People expected some scathing words at the preaching service which he was about to conduct, instead of which John Wesley preached a sermon on behalf of that particular charity and sent the treasurer the proceeds of a handsome collection.

On one occasion, at one of the early Conferences, there was a strong difference of opinion between John and Charles Wesley. Apparently, Charles Wesley lost his temper and threatened to leave. John Wesley, who always had his temper well under control no matter how provoked he was, said in a most matter-of-fact voice, "Give my brother his hat!"

John Wesley was always getting involved in controversies, though at heart he was really a peace-loving man. He was attacked again and again, in pulpits, on platforms and in scurrilous pamphlets. He could give as good as he got! On one occasion he said that his opponents "advanced arguments worthy of Bedlam and used language worthy of Billingsgate!"

John Wesley was riding to Northampton once, and overtook another rider, and they began to talk. The stranger held strong views on certain theological beliefs. John Wesley did not share these and tried to keep off discussing them. However, the other man persisted and in the end lost his temper and said, "I perceive you are one of the followers of John Wesley." "Oh no, I am not," was the instant reply. "I *am* John Wesley!" The other man on hearing this, would have liked to have ridden on, but John Wesley dryly writes: "Being the better mounted of the two, I kept close to his side, and endeavoured to show him his heart till we came into the street of Northampton."

Inimitable John Wesley!

XXV

HE ENDED GLORIOUSLY

ON one occasion, John Wesley said in his simple way, "Our people die well." When at the ripe old age of eighty-eight, honoured by rich and poor, high and low, his own turn came to pass into another life, those who were with him were able to bear witness to the fact that his end was not only peace, it was a triumphant finish to his splendid life of service and of witness.

There is a famous picture which now hangs at Wesley's Chapel, City Road, London, which shows a whole lot of people gathered round John Wesley's bed during his last moments. As a matter of fact, they could not all at the same time have got into his tiny bedroom. However, as they all came to see him during his last brief illness, the artist painted the room big enough to hold them all.

John Wesley kept going at top speed until he was sixty, and some folk thought that he would not be able to keep it up much longer. They were wrong. He continued to travel as cease-lessly as ever, to make new sermons as arresting as ever, and to publish new books as useful as ever. He used every waking moment in worth-while work for the Methodism that all the time was growing in numbers and in influence.

It was not until he was eighty-seven years old that John Wesley slowed down, and even then, he continued to preach, and though his sight was failing his mind was as eager and active as ever. He still got up very early, and one member of his big City Road family got up early too to read to him.

He preached at City Road for the last time on February 22, 1791. Two assistants had to support him in the pulpit, but people said that to see the radiant face of the old saint was a sermon in itself. Next day he went down to Leatherhead and preached there in the magistrate's room. There is a tablet on the spot now to commemorate that event. When, with difficulty, they managed to get the old veteran back to City Road, they knew that he would not last long. He got weaker and weaker but he could still sing! He surprised the tearful group around his bed by bursting out:

I'll praise my Maker while I've breath;
And when my voice is lost in death,
Praise shall employ my nobler powers.

It was a wonderful swan-song. He waved his hand and whispered, "The best of all is, God is with us," and then with a final "Farewell," John Wesley passed into the presence of the Master he had loved so much and served so well.

For a whole day his body lay in state in his own chapel at City Road, and thousands of his sad-eyed friends and followers filed past the simple coffin. The funeral was fixed for very early in the morning, as those responsible were afraid that there might be unmanageable crowds if the service were held at a more convenient time.

It was just like John Wesley to direct in his will, that at his funeral there should be "no

hearse, no coach, no escutcheon, no pomp."
Six poor men were to bear him to his last resting
place. That splendid, simple life was to have
an end splendid in its simplicity.

It is not too much to say that when he passed
home to God on March 2, 1791, at the age
of eighty-eight, he was *the* outstanding figure,
and *the* greatest force, in the English-speaking
world of that day. He had devoted himself
utterly to the service of his Lord; his gifts, his
time, his ease and his reputation. *Everything*
had been surrendered and everything had been
used to establish a work which during the past
two hundred years has gone from land to land
and from strength to strength.

It now remains for us all, old and young, to
carry into Methodism's third century
    the deep devotion,
       the selfless service,
          the high purpose and
             the dauntless courage
                of JOHN WESLEY.

XXVI

IT CAN HAPPEN TO YOU

EVERY year on May 24 ("Wesley Day"), millions,
yes *millions* of people think of the burdened and
worried little clergyman who went "'very un-

willingly" to Aldersgate Street on the evening of May 24, 1738. At "a quarter before nine" there comes a real thrill for all Methodists in England, America, Canada, Australia, South Africa, in fact all over the world, as they remember that it was at that precise moment more than two hundred years before, that John Wesley's heart was "strangely warmed." By ten o'clock you remember, with an elastic step, he was on his way to the lodging of his brother Charles to sing with him:

Where shall my wondering soul begin?

But those two brothers didn't just sing, and have a good time together, and then go on pretty much as before. If they had done that and no more, there would to-day have been no Methodism, in fact there would never have been any in 1738.

They wanted to get rid of everything evil in their own hearts, and they wanted to get an "assured belief" that God had forgiven them for all the wrong things in their lives. From that time on, they determined to love and to obey. Right to the end of their wonderful lives they spent every power they possessed in proclaiming to all Jesus—"the sinners' Friend" —and to them both was given the great joy of getting countless others to love and to obey.

Down through the two centuries, long after the passing of John and Charles Wesley, this

same thing has been going on in the Church
they left behind. People—old people, young
people, white people, coloured people—have
looked at Jesus Christ in His purity, then they
have looked into their own hearts and seen sin
there, and have wanted something better in its
place. They have prayed to God for a strength
greater than their own, and there has come to
them in different ways, and in so many different
places, the same "assured belief" that came to
the Wesleys. After that, these countless Methodists, all through the years, all over the world,
have continued to love and to obey, spending
their lives in happy fruitful service to God
and to their fellow men. It was to give people
this same satisfying peace and joy that Jesus
Himself came down to earth and lived and died,
and rose again.

And now, you who have been reading these
stories about John Wesley, where do you come
in? Where *will* you come in? It is the same Jesus
who was wanting to warm the hearts of John
and Charles Wesley, who wants you to experience the same joy and peace and usefulness that
was theirs.

John Wesley might have died a rich man,
which would have been a very poor thing to
have happened. As a matter of fact, he died
a very poor man, which was a splendid thing
to have happened; just what we should expect.

In his will, a very simple document, he left some of his few possessions to people whom he loved and who loved him, and then he signed his name and set his seal to the document. That seal is reproduced on page 95. You can see the rather ornamental initials, "J.W." and above them the words: BELIEVE LOVE OBEY.

John Wesley must have set tremendous store on those three words to have had them engraved on his seal. He must have thought that they were the very essence of Methodism—a way of life for all who should come into the circle of Methodism in days to come.

BELIEVE   LOVE   OBEY.

John Wesley's message and legacy from the eighteenth century to us in the twentieth, John Wesley's message and legacy to *you*. Will you take those three words of his into your thoughts, into your hearts, and into your lives? It doesn't matter how old you are or how young you are.

Make a drawing of John Wesley's Seal and mount it on a card. Above the seal write:

JOHN WESLEY'S HEART WAS WARMED
ON MAY 24, 1738.

Below the seal write:

I, TOO, WILL BELIEVE, LOVE AND OBEY,

and then add in your very best and firmest writing, your name and the date.

There is one further thing that you will probably find it helpful to do. As soon as you have signed the card, show it to some understanding person (somebody in your own home for choice), and ask that friend to help you keep your newly-made resolution.

And may the God of John Wesley bless you, every one of you, in the same way that he blessed John Wesley two centuries ago, with a peace and joy and usefulness that can be obtained only in one way.

It happened to John Wesley.

It can happen to YOU.

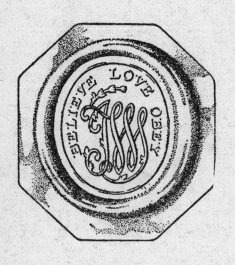